Robert Williams Buchanan

The Ballad of Mary the Mother

A Christmas carol

Robert Williams Buchanan

The Ballad of Mary the Mother
A Christmas carol

ISBN/EAN: 9783744796736

Printed in Europe, USA, Canada, Australia, Japan

Cover: Foto ©Thomas Meinert / pixelio.de

More available books at **www.hansebooks.com**

THE BALLAD OF MARY THE MOTHER

A Christmas Carol

BY

ROBERT BUCHANAN

"Say,—God is One, the Everlasting God; He begetteth not, and He is not begotten."—*The Koran.*

Λέγει αὐτῇ ὁ Ἰησοῦς. Τί ἐμοὶ καὶ σοί, γύναι.
—*John ii., 4.*

LONDON
ROBERT BUCHANAN
36, GERRARD STREET, SHAFTESBURY AVENUE, W.
1897

LONDON:
PRINTED BY A. BONNER,
1 & 2, TOOK'S COURT, CHANCERY LANE, E.C.

CONTENTS.

	PAGE
"Shepherds, wake, it is Christmas-tide . . . ."	vii
The Ballad of Mary the Mother	1
Ad Madonnam	103
A Catechism	115
Antiphones	127
L'Envoi	141
Prose Note	147

SHEPHERDS, wake, 'tis Christmas tide!
  (*Over the snow the bleak winds blow!*)
Follow, with yonder Star for guide,
  On Christmas day in the morning.

"The way is dark, the way is long,
We cheer the way with a blithesome song.

"Thro' the valley and over the hill,—
Hush, now hush, for the Star stands still!

"It stands so still and it shines so clear—
This is the place! Our Lord is here!"

Ye who have gifts, your gifts unfold—
Wood of Lebanon, gems, and gold.

Kneel, and shrive ye of your sin—
Then lift the latch, and enter in. . . . .

Alack, why stand ye weeping there? . . . .
" The fire is out, and the hearth is bare!

" Far have we wander'd thro' wintry gloom—
To seek His cradle, and lo! His tomb!

" Still overhead the Star shines clear,
But only the dust of the dead lies here:

" Ashes and dust in a frozen shroud,
Wherefore we wonder and weep aloud!

" Here he was born who long since died
   (Over the snow the bleak winds blow!)
Dark is the bield this wintertide
   On Christmas day in the morning."

THE BALLAD OF MARY THE MOTHER.

'Twas Mary, the woeful Mother,
   Came wandering footsore,
And stood, with her rags around her,
   Outside the synagogue door.

" O, who art thou, thou woeful woman,
   And what may thine errand be?"
" I am Mary, the Mother of thy Lord,
   And I come from Galilee."

" Stand back, stand back, whoever thou art,
   Thou canst not enter here,
Thy son is doing his Father's work
   Among his brethren dear.

" O woman, thou canst not enter now,"
   The grim door-keeper said,
" Thy son is pouring the Wine of Life,
   And breaking the holy Bread."

'Twas Mary the gentle Mother
　　Smiled, and laid bare her breast.
" 'Twas here he drank, and 'twas here he lay
　　Both waking and at rest.

" Go in, and tell him his Mother waits
　　Out here among the crowd "—
And as she spake, from far within
　　She heard him praying aloud.

'Twas one went in to the synagogue
　　When the deep prayer was done,—
" Rabbi, a woman is at the door :
　　Who saith thou art her Son.

" Her bare feet bleed from the thorny ways
　　'Twixt here and Galilee,
And with the woman thy brethren come,
　　And they would speak with thee."

The Lord stretch'd out his gentle hands
　　To his disciples dear :
" These are my mother, these are my brethren,
　　None else may enter here !

" I know no brethren, I know no mother,
  Save those who believe on Me!
Who eat with me of the Bread of Life
  My mother and brethren be!"

'Twas Mary, the woeful mother,
  Stood at the open door;
'Twas Jesus passed on his heavenward way
  And left her weeping sore.

His eyes were fixed on the far-off skies
  As he left her there bereaven,
He turned away from his mother's face
  To his Father's face in heaven.

As he wandered on from door to door
  She followed him from afar;
His face was bright as the moon in heaven,
  And hers like a lonely star.

It was Mary, the woeful Mother,
  Wept as she watched him go
Through the town, and up the height
  That looks on the sea below;

And his feet were as swift as the wind,
   And his eyes were as bright as fire,
And the face he turn'd to the shining Heaven
   Was wan with his heart's desire;

And his dress was of white, white wool,
   And his breast and his feet were bare,
And the light came down like his Father's Hand
   And lay on his golden hair!

And she heard his voice from afar
   Crying o'er land and sea:
" Father, my Father which art in Heaven,
   Shine down and strengthen me!"

* * *

It was Mary the woeful Mother
   Sat weeping on a stone,—
It was Mary, the dark-eyed Maiden,
   Found her weeping alone.

"Oh, why dost thou weep so sadly,
   And why is thy grey head bowed?"
(And the smile came through her great black eyes
   Like the light through a summer cloud).

"Rise up, thou weariful woman,
   Rise up and come with me—
Thou shalt sit this day in my palace bower
   And I will sit at thy knee;

"And when my maidens have wash'd thy feet,
   And the feast is over and done,
Thou shalt loosen thy lips and open thy heart
   And tell me of thy Son!"

It was Mary the woeful Mother
   Rose, weeping bitterlie,
And leaning on Mary the Maiden
   Hied to her bower by the sea.

As they walked through the fields of corn
   The birds were singing their song,
But the voice of the Lord above them
   Rang out more clear and strong;

And they saw the crowd on the mountain
   Gathering with glad acclaim,
And the Lord was standing above them
   And blessing those who came.

* * *

In the bower of Mary the Maiden
   There's a high seat and a low,
And the white robed serving maidens
   Are moving to and fro.

With dishes of gold and silver
   The banquet they prepare,
And the scent of myrrh and roses
   Is filling the air.

With white wine and with red wine
   The brimming gourds o'erflow;
And the Mother sits on the high seat,
   And the Maid on the seat below.

When the virgins have wash'd and anointed
   The weariful Mother's feet,
When over her head they have broken
   A box of ointments sweet;

When her mouth of the food hath eaten,
   And her lips have touched the wine,
She looketh on Mary the Maiden,
   And dryeth her tear-wet eyne.

"On thee and thine, my daughter,
   All peace and blessings be!
The God of Israël bless thee
   For thy sweet charitie!"

As fair as the Hûleh lily
   That blooms in the summer beam,
Was Mary the Maiden, wearing
   Her robe of the silken seam;

And on her hair and her bosom
   Were jewels and gems of price,
And round her neck there was hanging
   A charm with a strange device:

A heart of amber, and round it
   Ruby and emerald bands,
And over it, wrought in crystal,
   Two little wingëd hands!

White and warm was her bosom
  That rose and fell below,
And light on her face was playing,
  Deep, like the after-glow;

With the waves of her heaving bosom
  That strange light went and came,
Now dim and dark with the shadow of earth,
  Now flush'd with a heavenly flame;

And the warmth of the glad green meadows,
  The scent of the Night and the Day,
Flow'd up from Mary the Maiden
  To Mary the old and grey.

"O wherefore, my namesake Mary,
  Art thou so good to me,—
The woeful woman who wedded
  With Joseph of Galilee?

"Poor is my lot and lowly,
  Sad is my heart and sore,—
I am not worthy, my daughter,
  To enter thy palace door!"

'Twas Mary, the dark-eyed Maiden,
  The beautiful shining one,
Answer'd, "I love thee, Mother,
  For the Rabbi's sake, thy Son!

"To the fairest and best of mortals
  Thy womb hath given birth,—
Like the moon on the troubled waters
  He walketh the waves of Earth!

"White as a statue of marble
  Wrought in some Grecian land,
Fair as a palm-tree growing
  Green, mid the desert sand,

"Monarch of men he shineth
  Bright as the morning star,
A God, and of Godhead fashion'd,
  Not mortal as others are!

"There's a storm in my snow-white bosom
  Only his touch can still,—
There's a void in my heart, O Mother,
  Only his love can fill!"

'Twas Mary, the woeful Mother,
  Bent down and kissed her brow,
"God help thee, Mary, my daughter,
  And all such maids as thou!

" His love is not for the things of earth,
  His blessing for things of clay,—
A voice from a Land beyond the grave
  Is calling my Son away!

" How should he stoop to a love like thine
  Who hath no love for me?
In my womb he grew, from my womb he fell,
  And I nurst him on my knee."

'Twas Mary, the dark-eyed Maiden,
  Smiled through her night-black hair,—
" I met his eyes as he passed this day,
  And methought he found me fair!

" There is never a man of the sons of men
  Who would not smile on me,
But if thy Son is more than a man,
  Alack for me and thee!

"But if thy Son is Joseph's son,
 E'en as his brethren be,
Why, I am Mary of Magdala!
 And a King might mate with me."

'Twas Mary, the woeful Mother,
 Answered again, and said:
"The love of the world is not for him,
 Nor the happy bridal bed!

"He has cast away all women of earth
 Even as he casts out me,—
In my womb he grew, from my womb he fell,
 And I nursed him on my knee."

'Twas Mary, the dark-eyed Maiden,
 Frown'd, answering scornfullie—
"Nay, rather than be another's bride
 I would his leman be.

"Rather than mate with Herod the King
 Or Cæsar himself, his lord,
I'd be thy Son's, and ask no more
 Than a kindly look or word.

"I'd make my bed across his feet,
   I'd be his handmaiden,—
There is no other lord for me
   'Mong all the sons of men.

"Yea, though thy son be Joseph's son,
   Who toileth for his bread,
For one warm kiss of his rosy mouth
   Gladly I'd die," she said.

'Twas Mary the Mother answer'd:
   "Thy woe is even as mine;
Fain would I see my Son stoop down
   To a human love like thine.

"Hast thou not heard, O Mary,
   The wondering people say
'He is Moses or Eli risen again,
   Or a greater even than they'?

"Hast thou not heard them whisper low
   Who follow him night and day—
'The seed within his mother's womb
   Came from no human clay!'

" Hast thou not heard that, ere I wed
   My husband leal and true,
My womb was full of a wondrous life
   That quicken'd ere I knew;

" And how my mate was wroth and thought
   To thrust me from his side,
And how an Angel in the night
   Came to his bed and cried:

" *Forbear to know the woman thy wife,*
   Yet put her not away,
She is quick with child of the Holy Ghost.
   And hath known no man of clay;

" *Behold, it was written long ago,*
   Ere thy life's thread was spun,
'*A Virgin shall conceive of God,*
   Quicken, and bear a Son!' "

It was the dark-eyed Mary
   Sprang up her height and cried:
" Is this thing true, and is thy Son
   He that was prophesied?"

'Twas Mary, the Mother, raised her hands,
   And wept and tore her hair,—
" Woe worth the day that I was born,
   Or ever a child did bear !

" Hearken to me, my daughter,
   Sit down and hearken to me ;
But breathe not, out in the world of men,
   The thing I tell to thee.

" For the sands of my life run low,
   And the thread of my woe is out-worn,
And the Lord hath smitten the Mother down
   By the hand of her eldest born.

" 'Twas but a little hand
   When my babe lay here at rest,
A weak little hand, like a rose-leaf,
   That felt for my milky breast.

" Hearken to me, my daughter,
   And when my tale is done,
We'll kneel in the night together
   And pray for the man my Son ! "

* * *

Green leaf and blossom,
  White flower and red,
The whole world is gladdening
  Where Love's feet tread!

There's light in the morning,
  There's life for the young,
'Tis then the songs of Eden
  On every bough are sung!

The young maid is listening,
  Her lover by her side,—
Heaven the earth encircles,
  The bridegroom his bride.

Green leaf and blossom,
  White flower and red,—
The whole world is gladdening
  Where Love's feet tread!

* * *

" The God of Israël passeth
   From world to world on high,
The seas and the mighty mountains
   Quake as He passeth by;

" No eye hath looked upon Him,
   No soul hath fathom'd His ways,
His face is veil'd, though His breathing
   Filleth our nights and days;

" His Hand is a Hand in the darkness,
   His Voice is a Voice in the gloom,
But seed of Jehovah hath never
   Been sown in a woman's womb.

" Yet the Light that blindeth the vision
   Comes from the worlds He made,
And fire of the flesh He fashion'd
   Maketh the soul afraid.

"I wander'd happy and lonely
  By wood and meadow and stream,
And the joy of my youth was upon me
  And twined me away in a dream.

"And my love's voice said 'Thou art fairest,
  Thine eyes are the eyes of the dove,
Thy breasts are roses and lilies,'
  And I heark'd to the voice of my love!

"Yea, the joy of my life was upon me,
  And the light of my youth in my eyes,
And a breath like the breath of the morning
  Woke me in Paradise!

"By the beautiful waters of Marah
  We pitch'd our tent in the sun,
And we drank of the waters rejoicing,
  And, lo! our dreaming was done;

"For the taste of the waters was bitter,
  And the bright sun shone no more,
And I sat alone in the gloaming,
  And the day of my dream was o'er;

" Then I rose in my sorrow, casting
    Ashes and dust on my head,
For the seal of my womb was broken,
    And the flower of my youth had fled.

" Yet no one wist of the wonder
    As home to our house I came,
Only the God of our fathers
    Knew of His daughter's shame.

" And I dwelt in the house of my people
    And veil'd my face like a maid,
But ever when men came wooing
    I fled to my chamber and prayed.

" Morning and eve to the fountain,
    Between the night and the day,
I went with the village maidens
    Bearing my pitcher of clay.

" And a man from a neighbouring village
    Saw me, and thought me fair,
And, lo! when I journeyed homeward,
    I found him waiting there ;

"And while he spake with my father
    His eyes grew large on me;
And the man was stately and gentle,
    With a voice like the sough of the sea.

"And my father gave me unto him,
    With goats and kine for a dower,
And I fled to my lonely chamber
    And wept for many an hour.

"For the eye of my God was upon me
    While I wept and sorrow'd apart,
And a little hand in the darkness
    Was lifting the latch of my heart!

"Would I had died in the night-time,
    Would I had ne'er been born,—
I feared the eyes of the bridegroom,
    And sorrow'd from night till morn.

"Then came the hour of the bridal,
    The feast and the bridal song,—
O, weak is the heart of a woman,
    But the Law and the Lord are strong!

"As he bare me home to his dwelling
  'Twas summer in all the land,
But my heart was broken within me
  By the touch of that little hand.

"As we stood in the bridal chamber
  He offered me bread and wine,
And I feared the light of his loving
  As his eyes grew large on mine;

"And I fell at his feet, and weeping
  Pour'd out the gourd of my shame,
And the wrath of the Lord around him
  Like fireflaught went and came!

"And at first he hunger'd in anger
  To thrust me beyond his door,
But the mercy of God came on him
  Though his soul was stricken sore.

"And at last, when his wrath was over,
  His face grew gentle and mild,
And he spake as a gentle father
  Might speak to an erring child.

" O, blessings upon the bridegroom
    Who shielded his bride from wrong—
The heart of a woman is feeble,
    But the strength of a man is strong!

" The mighty God of our fathers
    Bless him in life or death,—
Wisest and best of mortals
    Was Joseph of Nazareth!

" He shielded me in my sorrow,
    He calm'd my spirit to rest,
He found the sheep that had wander'd
    And warm'd it on his breast.

" And when my travail was over,
    And the night of the birth-pang done,
He lifted the babe from my bosom
    And said, ' Behold our Son!'

" Yea, over the babe and the mother
    The balm of his love he poured,
And he named the new born JESUS,
    Which meaneth 'Sent by the Lord.'

"And I clave to my mate and master,
  The tenderest man among men,
Yea, I grew to his breast in gladness,
  His wife and his handmaiden!

"And after my cleansing he knew me,
  Yea, gave me the bridegroom's embrace,
And children were born unto us
  To gladden our dwelling place."

* * *

'Twas Mary, the grey-hair'd Mother,
   Bowed down her woeful head;
'Twas Mary, the dark-eyed Maiden,
   Reach'd up her arms and said:

" God's grace and blessing, Mother,
   Wrap thee from head to feet!
The ways of the world are weary,
   But the kiss of a mouth is sweet!

" Now tell me who was the lover
   Who brought thee such glad pain?
Some mighty lord of the City?
   Some chief of the lonely plain?"

'Twas Mary, the woeful Mother
   Moan'd to herself and said:
" His name will never be utter'd,
   Darkness hideth his head!

" He is gone like the dew of the morning,
　　He is fled with the flowers of the May,
His name on the sands of the desert
　　Was written and blown away.

" I clave to my lord and master,
　　And peace and joy were mine,
For the blissful milk of the mother
　　Flow'd in my breasts like wine;

" For the lips of my babe drew from me
　　The poison and the pain,
Till the weariful heart within me
　　Gladden'd and leapt again!

" A maid's love, O my daughter,
　　Is a pearl that men may buy,
But the love of a new-made mother
　　Is a rainbow in the sky!

" All peace of earth and of heaven
　　Are gather'd in her embrace—
Smiling the little one lieth
　　And looketh up in her face!

" His lips are lilies and roses,
    His scent is sweeter than myrrh,
He draweth bliss from her bosom
    And breatheth it back to her !

" Still as a star on my bosom
    My little first-born lay,
And like a fountain around him
    My love flow'd day by day !

" Clear as the summer heavens
    I saw his blue eyes shine !
Never on mortal bosom
    Shone babe so bright as mine !

" The days flow'd on like a murmuring brook
    That gladdeneth in the sun,—
For I heard the music of earth and heaven
    From the mouth of my little one !

" Brighter and fairer my first-born grew,
    And O, but it was sweet
To hold him up with a finger-touch
    When he stood upon his feet ;

"I could hold him up with a finger touch,
   He was so light and frail,—
But now he hath the might of a man
   How should my strength avail?

"Yet even in those sweet far-off days,
   So bright and now so dim,
Meseem'd the bairns his playfellows
   Were different from him!

"He seem'd not as other children
   That play in the summer beam,—
With the sound of their mirth around him
   He stood and look'd up in a dream!

"And while from hillock to hillock
   They flew with laugh and cry,
He watch'd the white clouds passing
   Over the still blue sky!

"So grave and yet so gentle,
   So still and yet so blest,—
It seemed some fountain of wonder
   Flow'd in his baby breast

" And one by one in the darkness
   The new-born waken'd and cried,
And I gladden'd, a fruitful Mother,
   Forgiven and purified!

" For lo! he gladden'd among them,
   The fairest and goodliest,
And still that fountain of wonder
   Flow'd in his gentle breast!

" And so he grew in the dwelling
   And brighten'd from day to day.
And the Light of the Lord was on us,
   And the Angels looked our way!"

* * *

There's a cry of little ones in the bield,
  And a patter of feet on the floor;
The Sun is splashing o'er farm and field
  To the golden pool at the door!
The earth is twining flowers in her hair,
  And there's some for you and me;
  Smile, Babe!—leap, Babe!—rock'd upon Mother's
    knee!

Of all the joys that the years can bring
  There is never a joy like this,—
Flowers to bloom, birds to sing,
  And the bud of a mouth to kiss!
Our goodman looks smiling on,
  And a proud goodman is he!
  Smile, Babe!—leap, Babe!—happy on Mother's knee!

Clear as a fountain by our fireside
  The cry of the young is heard,
Answer'd over the whole world wide
  By the cry of lamb and bird!
It's home-time now in the happy world,
   And it's Heaven with my bairns and me!
   Smile, Babe!—leap, Babe!—rock'd upon Mother's knee!

Round and around our house they run,
  A laughing, barefoot band—
Bright at the door the merry Sun
  With a golden nod doth stand!
And its oh! for the peace of Heaven and Home,
   And the light on my bairns and me!
   Smile, Babe!—leap, Babe!—happy on Mother's knee!

* * *

As the flower of the Hûleh lily
   Shineth after the rain,
The face of Mary the Mother
   Smiled, and grew bright again!

For the milk of the glad young mother
   Seem'd flowing in her breast,
And once again to her nipples
   A little mouth seem'd prest;

And her great grey eyes half closing
   Were dim with the happy dew,
And her red lips trembled and open'd
   As the quick glad breath came thro'!

" The peace of God was upon me,
   The smile of God at my door,
My soul was a summer fountain
   That filleth and floweth o'er!

" Fairer and fairer my first-born grew
    Till he was seven years old,
And his eyes had the glint o' the waters blue
    And his hair the sunset's gold.

" His voice was low as the voice o' the dove
    That cries in a shady place,
And the light of a love that was more than love
    Flowed from his shining face;

" For he loved all things that the Lord hath made,
    Who maketh great and small,
And he folded his little hands and prayed
    That God might guard them all!

" But ever of all God's creatures
    He loved the weak things best,—
The lamb that leaps in the meadows
    Would come and lie in his breast;

" The doves that dwell on the house-tops
    Would gather about his feet,
And the hungry dogs would lick his hands
    As he walk'd i' the sun-scorch'd street!

"And he loved the folk who were sick and weak,
    Whom God had stricken sore,
Yea, the tears would roll adown his cheek
    For pity of the poor;

"And sad was the heart of my little one,
    And his eyes grew wet and dim,
When the spotted lepers crawl'd i' the sun
    And held out hands to him! . . .

" In the synagogue of his fathers
    He heard the Rabbis preach,
And better than play or pleasure
    He loved their stately speech;

"Yea, even as the wild bee gathers
    Its honey from flower to flower,
He gathered the words of wisdom
    For many a happy hour.

"But best he loved (God bless him,
    And cherish him night and day)
The wandering men of the desert
    Who silently fast and pray.

" For when from the holy places
   One of these wights footsore,
With scoop of brass, and apron
   Of linen, would pass our door,

" My good man, merrily toiling
   Within at the carpenter's board,
Would bid the pilgrim enter
   And rest, in the name of the Lord;

" And when he had made ablution
   He'd enter and bless the place,
The silence of God around him,
   The light of God on his face;

" And Jesus would gaze upon him,
   Till he reach'd out hands and smiled,
And murmur'd, ' The God of Jacob
   Preserve the little child!'

" Then silently like a shadow
   He'd rise and wander away,
But the Light of God and His Silence
   Would dwell on the child all day."

* * *

" Oft, as he spelt his letters,
   Resting the scroll on my knee,
He'd close the scroll in his little hand
   And sigh, and question me—

" And 'twas 'Oh, mother,' and 'why, mother,
   Do mortals weary and die?
Surely our Father in Heaven
   Heareth his children cry?'

" The tales that a thousand mothers
   Tell to their sons, I told,—
Of the chosen race of Israël
   And the weariful days of old;

" And how in the land of bondage
   We wail'd beneath God's hand,
Till the prophet came to set us free
   And we gain'd the Golden Land;

" Dumbly he'd stand and listen
   While I those tales did tell,
And o'er and o'er he'd have me sing
   The psalms of Israël!

" O sweet he was as the summer rain
   That falleth on desert ways,
But ever the cry of human pain
   Troubled his nights and days!

" And 'twas ' O, mother,' and ' why, mother,
   Are folks so weary and sad?
The sick folk die, and the lepers cry,
   Though the sun shines bright and glad!'

" And he'd stand and muse apart,
   Like an old man bent with years,
And the well of wonder within his heart
   Fill'd, like an eye with tears!"

* * *

" And so my little one grew,
   The whitest lamb in the fold,
But the shadow dwelt in his eyes of blue
   And his ways were strange and old. . . .

" We came to the Holy City,
   And the streets were bright and gay,
And lo! from the hour my bairn was born
   'Twas thirteen years and a day.

" The Temple stood with its gates of gold
   On the heights of Jerusalem,
And the children gather'd like lambs i' the fold
   And the Elders question'd them;

"And we missed the child in the holy place,
   And wondering, sought for him,
And lo! he stood with a shining face
   In the halls of the Sanhedrim!

"And the Priests and Rabbis gathered round,
 And smooth'd their beards and smiled,
To hear the words of wisdom sound
 From the lips of a little child.

" Proud and glad was my heart that day
 For joy of the little one !
And blithe and merry we rode away
 When the Holy Feast was done ! . . .

" Stronger and fairer my first-born grew
 And in our bield he stayed,
For now he toil'd at the bench and knew
 My good man's gentle trade;

" And his voice chimed cheerily all day long
 To the chime of the busy plane,
And as I sat and heark'd to his song
 My heart was glad again !

" For methought ' My shame hath passed away,
 My son grows strong and tall,—
The God of Israël be his stay
 Wherever his feet may fall !

"The God of Israël grant him life
  And be his light and guide,—
And when he taketh a maid to wife
  May their seed be multiplied!

"'May their days be long in a fruitful land
  Under the summer skies,
And ere I sleep may he hold my hand
  And close my happy eyes.'

"O the light o' the Lord shone bright indeed
  Upon our dwelling place!
For methought my seed was a goodly seed
  To quicken and grow apace!

"And I saw my Son's seed multiply
  And gladden from day to day,
And I heard my children's children cry
  Like voices far away!

"The life of man is a tale thrice told,
  His joy is a flower full blown—
When our Son was nineteen summers old,
  He toil'd at the bench alone!

"The weight of years on his hair so grey,
   The sleep-dust in his eyne,
My good man Joseph passed away
   While I held his hand in mine;

"Gently he beckoned the first-born near
   And gazed in his face and said:
'O, Jesus, look to thy mother dear
   When I lie cold and dead!'

"'Twas darkness then in the lowly bield
   For many and many a day;
For he who had been my strength and shield
   Was taken and hid away.

"My children gathered around my knee
   And I bowed my widow'd head,
But gently my first-born smiled on me
   And my grief was comforted.

"O, blessed be the name of the Lord!
   He taketh and giveth again,
His wrath is fire and a flaming sword,
   But His love is summer rain;

' The flesh of the stricken He healeth up,
   The sick He maketh sound,—
When our grief is full as a brimming cup
   He poureth it on the ground.

" The peace of God on my spirit fell
   For joy of the man my Son,—
At his father's board he wrought full well
   Till his daily task was done.

" There was never a man of woman born
   Was half so fair as he,—
Like the sound of a fountain night and morn
   Was the voice of my Son to me.

" And evermore when his toil was o'er
   He loved to wander away,
To comfort the sick and cheer the poor,
   Or to muse apart and pray.

" And in the synagogue he'd teach
   Among the Rabbis old,
And he gather'd wisdom, and lo, his speech
   Grew stranger twentyfold;

"But ever I murmur'd day and night,
  'Never was Son like mine;
O, may his days be long and bright,
  And his flesh a fruitful vine.'"

* * *

"Out of the lonely desert
   Preaching Jochanan came,
And stood in the shallows of Jordan
   Naming the one God's Name.

"Wild as the horse of the desert
   No man may saddle and ride,
Over his naked shoulders
   A cloak o' the camel's hide;

"He cried aloud to the people,
   Who gather'd on the strand,
'Repent! repent; for the Kingdom
   Of Heaven is close at hand!'

"And men and women and children,
   From morn to evenfall,
Flock'd to the Prophet's bidding
   And he baptised them all;—

"With water he baptised them
  Under the open sky,
And lo! on the second morning
  The man, my Son, stood nigh!

"And lo! as they met together
  The eyes of John were dim,
For as morning star unto evening star
  Was the man, my Son, to him!

"Yet with water he baptised him,
  And lo, when it was done,
The hunger and thirst of Godhead
  Grew in the soul of my Son;

"And he wandered away from the people
  Into a desert place,
And there alone with the Silence
  He fasted and hid his face;

"And the stars of Heaven beheld him,
  And the wild beasts hovered near,
But the eye of man did not see him
  And the ear of man did not hear;

"And he ate not and he drank not,
  But fasted and prayed, and so
The flesh on his bones was wasted,
  And the light of his life burnt low.

"And when I again beheld him
  I trembled and sobbed aloud,
For the dews of Death were upon him
  And his face seem'd set in a shroud!

"'O where hast thou been, my Jesus,
  And why is thy look so wild?'
He stood like a ghost in the doorway
  And lookt in my face and smiled;

"And his smile was loving and gentle,
  Tho' his face was ashen grey,
But his eyes were gazing through me
  At something far away!

"'O where hast thou been, my Jesus,
  And what didst thou hear and see?'
'I heard the winds of the night,' he said,
  'And the Silence spake to me!'

"'Alas and alas, my Jesus,
   And what didst thou see and hear?'
'I saw the Dead in their shrouds pass by,
   And the Souls of the Dead stood near!

"'And I heard the beasts of the desert
   Moaning like human things,
And the Spirit of Darkness cover'd my head
   And wrapt me 'neath his wings.

"'But I knelt and prayed that my Father in heaven
   Would shrive me of my sin,
And the Gates of Heaven swung open wide
   To show the lights within;

"'And a Face looked out of the Golden Gates,
   And the Spirit of Darkness fled,
And the hand of God like a Father's Hand
   Was placed upon my head.

"'And the Voice of God, like a Father's voice,
   Came down the dark to me,—
"Go forth, go forth in thy Father's Name,
   For He hath chosen thee."'

"'Alas, and alas, my Jesus,
   What didst thou see and hear?
The words thou speakest are dark and strange,
   And fill my soul with fear.

"'The Master of Earth and Heaven
   Hath neither feet nor hands,—
The wind of His breath is as the blast
   That bloweth the desert sands.

"'His face no eye hath looked on,
   His voice no ear hath heard,—
And yet his face is the Light o' life,
   And His voice is a wingëd Word.'

"Sadly he gazed upon me,
   With great eyes dim with pain,
And the face of my Son burn'd bright through tears,
   Like a rainbow through the rain.

"'Come in and rest, my Jesus,
   Thy spirit is weary and worn,
Come in and sleep in thy father's house
   Where thou, my child, wast born;

" 'And I, thy mother, will sit beside
   Thy bed, and sing to thee
The song I sang when I sang and rock'd
   Thy cradle with my knee.'

" Sadly he gazed upon me,
   Folding his hands in prayer,—
' My Father's House is wide as the world,
   And high as the heavens up there.

" ' My Father's House is wide as the world,
   And I was born therein,—
My Father calleth me out of Heaven
   To cleanse it of its sin.

" ' Never again shall my Father's Son
   Rest in a narrow bed,—
To and fro, and up and down,
   His weariful feet must tread.

" ' Never again shall my Father's Son
   Hark to thy cradle song,—
To and fro, and up and down,
   He goes, for the way is long.'

"'Hearken to me, my Jesus,
   Stay, and hearken to me:
Thy sisters and brethren who sit within
   Would break their bread with thee.

"'Come in, come in, and sit at the board,
   Where my first-born should be,
And I, thy mother, will wash thy feet,
   And stand and wait on thee!'

"Sadly he gazed upon me,
   Frowning he turned away,—
'Who break with me the Bread of Life,
   My sisters and brethren are they!

"'No brethren dwell in my Father's House
   Save those who eat His Bread,
No mother's love can save the quick
   Or wake and shrive the dead!

"'And woe is me for my brethren dear
   Who o'er the wide world stray,
And woe is me for the witless love
   That withereth in a day!

"'Lo, there be beds in my Father's house
  Many as waves o' the sea,—
From bed to bed my feet must pass
  Till the sleepers wakened be!

"'Lo! there be boards in my Father's house
  Where men feast merrily,—
From board to board my feet must pass
  Till all shall follow Me!'

"He turn'd away with a weary moan
  From the bield where he was born,
And as he wander'd from door to door
  His townsfolk laughed in scorn!

"For strange he seemed as a witless wight
  Whose soul and sense are dim,
And his eyes were bright with a vacant light,
  And the children mock'd at him!

"We followed him slowly as up the street
  Slowly he went his way,
And we saw him enter the Synagogue,
  For 'twas the Sabbath day;

" And silently he enter'd in
   And stood in the midst o' the crowd,
And his head was raised as they named the
      Name,
   Tho' all the rest were bowed !

" And he took the scroll in his thin white hand
   While the Elders gather'd round,
And he read the lesson, and named the Name,
   And sat down to expound ;

" The first words that he utter'd there
   Were gentle and soft and low,
And the sound of his voice was as the sound
   Of a fountain's ebb and flow ;

" The next words that he utter'd there
   Were wild and strange and loud,
And the sound of his voice was as the sound
   Of the riven thunder-cloud ;

" The next words that he utter'd there
   Were drown'd in fierce acclaim,
For the Elders rose and tore their beards
   And the folk shriek'd out in shame !

" Around my Son like an angry sea
   They gather'd shrieking shrill,
And his face was calm as a patient star
   And his pale lips murmur'd still :

" Again he utter'd the Name of Names,
   Nor knelt on bended knee,
But his eyes looked up as if they saw
   The Face no man may see.

" With curses and blows they thrust him forth
   Into the open street,
And spectral pale he stood at the door
   Like a corpse in his winding sheet.

" ' Come home, come home, my Jesus,
   Come home with me,' I cried,
And gently I sought to guide him home,
   But he pushed my hand aside.

" ' No home have I but my Father's Home,
   And thither my feet must fare,—
My Father's Home is as wide as the world,
   And high as the heavens up there.' "

* * *

Thou shalt not see, thou shalt not hear,
Yet I, the Lord thy God, am near.

Thou shalt not hear, thou shalt not see,
Yet I, thy God, abide with thee.

My spirit stirs around thee (saith
The Lord) thy nostrils drink my breath.

So near am I both night and day,
And yet my throne is worlds away.

Seek not to unveil or fathom Me,—
But shut thine eyes, and bend thy knee.

Juggle not with the Law Divine,
Nor seek my Heavens for a sign.

I am veil'd for ever, I am dumb,
And yet my thunders go and come.

*Father and Lord I am indeed,
And yet have neither Son nor seed.*

*Thou shalt not hear, thou shalt not see,
Yet I, thy God, abide with thee.*

*Let it suffice thee that I reign,—
Beware to take my Name in vain.*

*Go then thy ways,—though I am near,
Thou shalt not see, thou shalt not hear.*

* * *

It was Mary the woeful Mother
   Cried, weeping bitterlie,
" My days are dark, for the Lord my God
   Hath taken my Son from me!

" He walked by the lonely waters,
   And saw the ships go by,
And he cried aloud, and the men o' the ships
   Heard, and answer'd his cry!

" And the sound of his voice could still the pain
   In the hearts of the tempest-blown,
For he spoke of the waters no ship may gain
   And the land no man hath known!

" And the men o' the sea forsook their nets
   And, gathering one by one,
Sat by the waters of Galilee
   And heark'd to the man, my Son.

" And his voice was soft as the rain
  That falleth cool on the grass,
And his face was like the moon in the sky
  That watches the Tempest pass!

" And the souls of the men o' the sea
  Close to my Son did creep,
And he reached out hands and counted them
  As a Shepherd counteth his sheep!

" Alone I bode in the lonely house
  And his blessing reached not me,—
I heard his voice like a sea-bird's cry
  Far out on a sunless sea!

" And the Elders flocking about our house
  Cried, ' Woe to him and thee!
The mad folk gather to hear thy Son
  And his mouth speaks blasphemy!

" ' He prophesieth and raveth loud
  Out there by Galilee,
With woven hands and with magic spells
  He lures the men o' the sea!

"'He eateth and drinketh unpurified,
  He breaketh the Sabbath day;
He is Eli or Moses risen, he saith,
  Or a greater even than they!'

"Nay then, the words they spake were sore
  For a mother's ear to hear,
And I cried: 'He is holy and pure of heart,
  And such to the Lord are dear!

"'Fair as a lily-flower, my Son
  Hath grown to the height of man—
Ah, never yet grew a flower so fair
  On earth, since the earth began!'

"Yet ever the wonderful rumour grew,
  And men began to tell
Of mighty magic in secret wrought
  Wherever my Son's foot fell:

"How the lame man walked, and the blind man
    saw,
  And the dumb man spake and heard,
How the waxen man laid out for dead
  Had bitten his shroud and stirred!

"Nay, then my heart was sick with fear
    And I feared for the man my Son,
For I wist such wonders are often wrought
    By will of the Evil One!

"'He casteth down Devils by Belzebub,
    Who is Prince of Devils,' they said,
And I turn'd my face to the wall, and cast
    Ashes and dust on my head.

"For my buried shame had risen again
    And haunted my soul forlorn,
As I prayed for the soul of the man, my Son,
    Even Jesus my first-born.

"Suddenly through the streets o' the town
    I heard the laugh and the cry,
And follow'd by throngs of stranger folk
    Jesus, my Son, went by.

"And those who follow'd were ragged and poor,
    And many were gaunt and gray,
And I cried his name as he passed our door
    But his face was turned away.

" And the townsfolk mock'd him as he walked
    Swiftly from street to street,
But when he came to the edge o' the town
    He shook the dust from his feet.

" ' Never was Prophet honoured yet
    By those of his own countrie,—
Woe to the town where I was born
    And the folk who mock at me!'

" And he wandered up and over the hills,
    And his feet were swift as wind,
And I join'd the throng o' the sick and poor
    That crept and crawl'd behind;

" And down to the shore of the lonely Sea
    Of Galilee he came,
And the throngs of woeful women and men
    Gather'd and called his name."

* * *

It was Mary the gentle Mother
　　To Mary the Maiden cried,—
" Like waves o' the sea, the people
　　Flow'd on the mountain side;

" And even as a rock in the waters
　　The man, my Son, stood there,
And the light of the still blue Heaven
　　Slept on his golden hair.

" When he reached out hands and bless'd them,
　　They were hush'd as waves o' the sea,
And their faces were dark with yearning
　　As they listen'd on bended knee;

" For his voice was sweet as a fountain
　　Or the voice of the turtle dove,
As he told of a Heavenly Kingdom
　　And the love that is more than love;

"And the burden of earth was uplifted
  By the touch of a magic hand,
And the folk beheld as they hearken'd
  The gleam of the Promised Land:

"A land of milk and of honey,
  Golden and bright and blest,
Where the wicked would cease from troubling
  And the weary would be at rest!

"Then the peace of God flowed round me
  And the days of my woe seemed done,
As I listened happy and smiling,
  To the voice of the man, my Son!

"Kind were his words and gentle,
  Bright was his face and mild,—
Happy he seem'd and loving
  As when he was a child!

"'Come to me, ye who hunger,
  Come, and be straightway fed!
For lo! I bring from the Father
  Not ashes and dust, but bread!

"'Come to me, ye who are weeping,
   And all your tears shall cease,
For lo! I bring from the Father,
   Not trouble and pain, but peace!

"'Come to me, ye who are stricken,
   Who sicken and fight for breath,
For lo! I bring from the Father
   Eternal Life, not Death!'

"Sweet as a fountain's falling
   The music filled our ears:
'Your Father in Heaven loves you
   And fain would dry your tears!

"'Your loving Father in Heaven
   Heareth his children's cries—
Let him who is sick, then, gladden,
   Let him who hath fallen rise!'

"And the wind of his words went swiftly
   Over the wondering crowd,
And like waves of the sea uprising
   They wept and they sob'd aloud!

" Then one shriek'd loudly 'Rabbi!
　　Heal me, lest I die!'
And lo! with a thousand voices
　　They echo'd that woeful cry!

" Ragged, and worn, and weary
　　They gathered under the skies,—
And the blind men groped unto him
　　Rolling their sightless eyes!

" And the little afflicted children
　　Close to his knees upcrept,
But the lepers stood afar off
　　And reach'd out hands and wept!

" Pale as a man of marble
　　He stood on the lone hillside,
And wept as he gazed upon them,
　　And lifted up hands and cried:

" 'The Light I bring from the Father
　　Shineth in secret ways,—
Only the Hand that smiteth
　　And slayeth, hath power to raise!

"'And yet the sick shall be healéd,
   And the blind shall surely see,
For my Father's door is open
   To those who follow me!

"'Weep not, but be of comfort!
   Fret not, your woes shall cease!
For lo! I bring from the Father
   Love, and exceeding Peace!'

"But still they gather'd and murmur'd
   With piteous woes and cries:
And the blind cried, 'Master, heal us!'
   Rolling their sightless eyes!

"But e'en as they flock'd around him
   And reached out hands and cried,
He girded up his raiment
   And passed from the mountain side.

"Swift through the clamouring people
   He walked, nor gazed on them,
While they thronged to look upon him
   And to touch his raiment hem;

"And the blind folk groped in the sunlight,
　And the sick folk wept in woe,
And the lepers gazed from afar off
　And wail'd, as they watched him go!"

* * *

'Twas Mary, the dark-eyed Maiden,
    Reach'd out her hands and cried:
"These things thou sawest, O Mother,
    These things and nought beside?

"Was not the sick man healéd?
    Did not the blind man see?
Such wonders were wrought, 'tis rumour'd,
    Out yonder by Galilee!"

'Twas Mary the woeful Mother
    Answer'd in soul's despair,—
"Woe worth the day that I was born
    Or ever a Son did bear!

"How shall the hand of a mortal
    Give back what God hath ta'en—
If the hand of a man could dry our tears
    No man would weep again!

"The sick would sicken no longer,
  The blind would gladden and see,—
But man is dust, and what God hath bound
  No man that is dust shall free! . . .

"When darkness over the mountain
  Fell, for the day was done,—
Silently down the mountain side
  I followed the man my Son;

"And I found him standing alone,
  On the shore of a stormy sea,—
With hair and raiment backward blown
  He prayed, and he marked not me;

"And his hands were raised to the sky
  Where the angry storm-clouds drave,
'Father, Father,' I heard him cry,
  'Stretch down thy hand and save!

"'That the blind may see, that the sick be heal'd,
  That my word may wake the Dead!'
And the storm roll'd on, and the thunders peal'd,
  And the lightning flash'd and fled.

"'Father, Father, if I indeed
   Thy dread commandments keep,
Help me to heal the hearts that bleed,
   To dry the eyes that weep.

"'Wearily over the whole world wide
   My stricken brethren lie;—
Father in Heaven, look down,' he cried,
   'Succour them, since they die!'

"And, lo! he fell on his face and prayed
   Alone on the lone sea-shore,
And I watch'd him, trembling and afraid,
   Till he stirred and rose once more.

"And, lo! the storm of the night had fled,
   Softly the night-wind blew,
And the clouds were opening overhead,
   And the stars were shining through.

"And the light, like a hand snow-white,
   Lay on his golden hair,
As he walked on the shore at the dead o' night
   And found me waiting there.

"Face to face in the silence
   We stood by the sleeping sea,—
'Woman,' he said, 'what brings thee here,
   And wherefore seekest thou Me?'

"Then my heart broke in my bosom,
   And I sank on my bended knee,—
'I am Mary, thy Mother, and all night long
   My tears have flowed for thee.

"'I heard thy voice on the mountain side
   Sweet as the wood-dove's cry,
And the doors of Heaven seemed opening wide
   And the Spirit of God went by!'

"Gently he gazed upon me
   As I knelt upon my knee,—
'God bless thee, Mary, my Mother,
   Dost thou believe on Me?

"'I have prayed, and my prayer is answer'd,
   I have wept, but my tears are done,
My Father in Heaven hath heard my prayer,
   And, lo! we twain are One.

"'Even as the love of the Father
   The love of the Son shall be;
Even with the hands of the Father
   The Son shall set men free.

"'Greater than I is the Father,
   And yet we twain are One!'
Weeping I rose to my feet and gazed
   In the face of the man, my Son.

"'Alas, alas, my Jesus!
   Thy riddle is hard to read,—
The God of Israël dwelleth afar,
   And hath neither Son nor seed!

"'No eye of a mortal fathom can
   The waters of Death and Doom,—
Seed art thou of a mortal man,
   And grew in thy mother's womb!

"'Come home, come home, my Jesus,
   And dwell in peace with me—
The Lord is the Lord of Heaven and Hell,
   Thy mother hath only thee.'

" Sadly he gazed upon me,
  Frowning he turn'd away,
'Woe to thee, woman of little faith,
  In the dawn of my Judgment Day!

"'I have no brethren, I have no mother,
  Save those who believe on Me!
Son of my Father am I, and no other
  Judgeth the lost, and thee!'

" Sadly he gazed upon me
  With eyes all woe-begone,
Full of the hunger of Godhead
  That gleam'd in the eyes of John!

" But when I clutched at his raiment,
  He wept and turned from me,
And passed on shipboard, and sailed away
  With the wild-eyed men o' the sea;

" And his voice rang out once more
  From the deck of the ship, and lo!
The sick and blind flocked down to the shore,
  And wail'd as they watch'd him go!

" And swiftly into the Night
   He flew, as a sea-bird flies,
And the lepers gathered upon the height,
   And wail'd to the empty skies."

* * *

The Leper said:
"Lord God, if thou art just,
Heap earth upon my head,
  Bury me, dust to dust!
I did not crave to be,
  Yet lo, I crawl i' the sun,
And if Thou healest not me,
Slay me and set me free—
  So let Thy Will be done!"

The Blind Man said:
"Lord God, I seek the Light—
Wherever my cold feet tread,
  'Tis night, eternal night.
Darkly I've sought for Thee,
  Dear Lord, since life begun,
But since I still must be,
God, give me eyes to see—
  So let thy Will be done!"

The Mad Man said:
 Lord God, uplift thy hand!
Demons and spectres dread,
 Fill me at thy command!
I loathe Thy works and Thee,
 O thou Almighty One,
I did not crave to be—
Slay me, or set me free,
 So let thy Will be done!"

God said:
 " Peace! for your cry is vain,—
I weave of quick and dead
 An ever lengthening chain.
Peace! from my Law and Me
 No man escapeth,—none,—
Long as the earth and sea
Endure, these things shall be,—
 For so my Will is done!"

* * *

'Twas Mary the gentle Mother
   Listen'd with lips apart,
While the voice from the lonely mountain
   Flow'd thro' her empty heart.

"Fairer he is and gentler
   Than other mortals be,
But his thoughts are yonder in Heaven,
   Not here on the earth with me.

"I would to God he were lying
   A babe on my breast this day,—
The light of his eyes is the light o' love,
   But it shineth so far away!

"I hear a voice still crying
   Aloud to the sons of men,
But the cry of the babe on my bosom
   Will never be heard again!

"Rabbi the people call him,
  Rabbi and Master and King;
He breaketh bread on the mountain,
  While I sit famishing!"

'Twas Mary, the dark-eyed Maiden,
  Gazed from the bower and said:
"He healeth the spots of the Leper,
  He raiseth up the Dead!

"And lo! as he passeth the gateway
  With ragged throngs behind,
Out of the lanes are crawling
  The sick and the halt and the blind;

"E'en as a King of the people
  He passeth on his way,
And whoso toucheth his raiment-hem
  Is straightway healed, they say!

"Their bread he multiplieth,
  He turneth their water to wine—
Surely this Man, O Mother,
  Is more than flesh of thine?"

'T was Mary, the woeful Mother,
   Bowed down her head and cried,—
"The God of Israël bless him
   From morn to eventide!

"Flesh of my flesh, O Mary,
   Bone of my bone, is he,—
In my womb he grew, from my womb he fell,
   And I nursed him on my knee.

"From place to place he passeth,
   Stately and tall, like one
Who walketh on thrones to his kingdom,
   And yet . . . he is my Son!

'Gladly my soul would greet him
   Though he were thricefold King,
But ever behind him as he walks
   The Shadow is following!

"Man is a spark in the darkness,
   His days are only a breath,
The wings of the Lord are wide as the world
   And the shadow thereof is Death."

'Twas Mary, the grey-haired Mother,
   Rose trembling on her feet—
"The ways of the world are many,
   But yonder, all ways meet!

"The wings of the Lord are mighty
   And shadow all things that be,—
I hear their sound in the silence
   Deep as the sound of the Sea.

"The heart of the Temple is cloven,
   The high-priest waileth aloud,
The wrath of the Lord is growing,
   Black as the thunder-cloud.

"The rose and the Hûleh lily
   Bloom but a little space,—
After his day man sleepeth,
   Alone in a lonely place.

"Never the dead that sleepeth
   Shall slip his shroud and rise—
His ears are sealéd for ever,
   Darkness filleth his eyes."

Twas Mary, the dark-eyed Maiden,
　　Stood at the gate and cried :
" O, hark! they hail him as sent of God,
　　Promised and prophesied ! "

'Twas Mary, the woeful Mother,
　　Stood up and tore her hair :
" Woe worth the day that I was born
　　Or ever a son did bear.

" The God of Israël crieth
　　' There is no God save Me ! '
The Elders of Israel gather in wrath
　　Like waves of a stormy sea."

'Twas Mary, the dark-eyed Maiden,
　　Gazed from the gate and cried :
" Thy Son shall wear a crown on his head,
　　Yea, and a sword at his side.

" The people cry he is Lord and King,
　　Though he be Son of thine,—
O would that I were the Queen o' the King,
　　Or even his concubine !

"There is never a man of the sons of men
    Who is half so fair as he,—
Be he seed of a mortal, or son of God,
    He is Master of men and me."

'Twas Mary the woeful Mother
    Sank to her knees and said:
"Look forth, look forth, and tell me now
    Whither my Son's feet tread?"

'Twas Mary the dark-eyed Maiden
    Laughed merrily, answering:
"His face is turned to Jerusalem,
    And there they will crown him King.

"Be he seed of a mortal or son of God,
    The folk will crown him there."
'Twas Mary the Mother shrieked aloud,
    And wept and tore her hair!

"I hear a Voice he cannot hear,
    That crieth 'Forbear! forbear!'
I see a Hand he cannot see
    That holdeth a sword in the air!

"The Elders of Israël gather in wrath
   Like waves of a stormy sea!
The God of Israël crieth aloud,
   'There is no God but Me!'

"The God of Israël crieth aloud
   As He to our fathers cried—
'The soul of a man is the breath of a mouth,
   But I, the Lord, abide!'"

* * *

The Lord and the Law are One
   And nought can sunder them!
Wherever their swift feet run
   The worlds rock under them!

Wherever the Lord hath past
   The Law fulfilleth Him,
E'en Death lies low at last,
   For a mightier stilleth him!

One, the Law and the Lord,
   That passes and interpasses,
Sure, as the sweep of a sword,
   Still, as the growth of the grasses!

Two, yet ever the same,
  Life and Death for their token,—
The Lord that hath no name,
  And the Law ne'er broken!

No miracles come of these
  Whose miracles are for ever,
Their mystery no man sees,
  It is uttered never.

Life and Death and Birth
  Betoken their ministration,
On the Earth, and over the Earth,
  And through all Creation.

The Law and the Lord are One,
  And nought can sunder them!
Wherever their Will is done,
  All things bow under them!

Think not with prayer or praise,
  When the grave gapes wide for thee,
To stop the sun on its ways
  Or turn God aside for thee!

He is Lord to the furthest sun,
 With his strength He thrilleth him,
But the Law and the Lord are One,
 And his Work fulfilleth Him!

* * *

As they parted his raiment among them,
   For his vesture casting lots,
On the clouds of the night burnt brands of light
   Like crimson leper-spots;

But the storm of the night was over
   And the wild winds ceased to cry,
Yea, all was still on the skull-shaped hill
   As the Spirit of Death crept by.

'Twas Mary the woeful Mother
   Lay prone beneath the Tree,
And Mary the Maid knelt down and prayed
   With Mary of Bethany.

And the light came out of the skies
   And struck the Cross on the hill . . .
And Jesus moaned and open'd his eyes,
   And the heart of the world stood still !

On his head the thorny crown,
   His body bleeding and bare,
He woke on the Cross, and gazing down
   Beheld his Mother there!

And "Mother! Mother dear!"
   He murmured smiling sweet,—
And Mary arose, and creeping near
   Sobbed, and embraced his feet.

And "Mother! Mother dear!"
   Softly he sighed again,
And over his wounds, as she sobbed to hear,
   Her wild tears ran like rain!

Not to his Father in Heaven,
   Not to the empty skies,—
To Mary the Mother he looked, and no other
   Blest, with his dying eyes.

The love of the Lord of Heaven
   Is a dream that passeth by,
But the love of a mortal Mother
   Is a love that doth not die!

The sword of the Lord of Heaven
  Husheth his children's cry,
But the love of a mortal Mother
  Shines on, tho' God goes by!

Gently he gazed upon her
  Who had loved him last and first,—
Then darken'd again with the cruel pain,
  And murmur'd low, "I thirst!"

As they set the sponge on a spear
  And moisten'd his mouth, he said,
Smiling down on his mother dear,
  "Lo, it is finishéd!"

And he bowed his head on his breast
  And utter'd a woeful cry,
And the weariful Mother's lips were prest
  To his wounds,—while God went by!

* * *

'Twas Mary, the happy Mother,
   Smiled and knelt on her knee,
And bared her breast and opened her arms
   As they drew him down from the Tree.

She pillow'd his head on her bare breast-bone
   And gave him kisses three—
" In my womb he grew, from my womb he fell,
   God giveth him back to me!"

And over the cold still waxen face
   Rain'd down her locks o' grey,
And the heavens were black, but the gates of Heaven
   Were opening far away;

And the birth-star looked from the gates o' Death
   As she rock'd the corse on her knee,
And the Earth lay silently down to watch
   In the still bright arms o' the Sea.

On the breast of Mary the Mother
   He rock'd beneath the Tree,
And Mary the Maiden sat at his feet
   With Mary of Bethany;

And, lo! they croon'd his cradle-song
   As she rock'd him on her knee,—
There was Mary the Mother, and Mary the Maiden,
   And Mary of Bethany.

'Twas Mary, the woeful Mother,
   Wept as she sang, and cried:
"My little one sleeps upon my breast,
   For, lo! 'tis the eventide.

"And round and round my cold breast-bone
   I feel the white milk stir!"
And she wept aloud, and the Maries twain
   Wept, and drew close to her.

"Now dry thine eyes, O Mother dear,
   Smile and be comforted,—
Thy Son doth sleep, but thy Son shall wake
   To judge both Quick and Dead.

"Thy Son hath promised to wake again,
   And the folk shall bring his crown,—
The clay thou nursest is not thy Son,
   But thy Son is looking down."

'Twas Mary, the woeful Mother,
   Pressed tight her mouth to his:
"My Son is sleeping upon my breast,
   And his red, red mouth I kiss.

"By the milk that stirreth around my heart
   I know my little one;
By the flesh that was woven in my womb I know
   The flesh and the bone of my Son.

"I hold him now, I clasp him now,
   He is mine for evermore,
For the sun hath sunken upon his wrath,
   And the day of his Dream is o'er.

"Never more will he open his eyes
   To waken and weep!
Never more will the wind and the rain
   Trouble his sleep!

"The heart of the Temple is cloven,
   The High Priest teareth his hair,
But God is good, He giveth me back
   The fruit that my womb did bear!

"Yea God is good, for my Son is mine
   To cherish and clasp and keep,—
And I too, holding him in my arms,
   Shall croon myself to sleep!"

'Twas Mary the bright-eyed Maiden
   Rose up her height and cried:
"The womb of the night is cloven with light!
   He liveth, and hath not died!

"He liveth, Lord and Master of men,
   And he shall rise and reign!
For man is dust, and the hand of a man
   Smiteth at God in vain!"

'Twas Mary the woeful Mother
   Raised up her face and cried:
"Go by! the seal of thy God lies here
   On the lids of the Crucified!

"Go by, for I loved my child too well
   To bid him waken and weep—
My God is good, and the hand of God
   Giveth my little one sleep!"

'Twas Mary of Bethany weeping cried,
   "Hush, for I hear a tread!
They're coming hither over the hill
   To seek and bury the dead;

"And one uplifteth a torch on high
   To light them as they go,
And they who follow are bearing a shroud
   Of linen white as snow!"

* * *

And now they've embalm'd his white bodie
   With myrrh and spices sweet,
And round and round they've lapt the folds
   Of the long, long winding sheet;

And they've bound up tight his bearded chin
   With waesome linen bands,
And over his frozen breast they've spread
   His yellow waxen hands;

And they've borne him up to the black hillside
   To his lonesome Sepulchre,
And they've set him down in the narrow place,
   And still he doth not stir . . . .

" Now come away, thou woeful woman,
   And leave him sleeping alone,
Let us close the mouth of his Sepulchre
   And seal it with a stone!"

94 THE BALLAD OF MARY THE MOTHER

'Twas Mary the Mother kissed his cheeks
    And sobbed in soul's despair,—
And the torchlight lay like a bloody hand
    Upon her poor grey hair.

And from over the hill the stars looked down
    With dim sad tearful eyes,
For the cry of the Mother's broken heart
    Rang through the empty skies.

(It rang to the foot of the Throne of God
    Where all the wide world's woe,
The dole of a million broken hearts,
    Melts like a flake of snow.)

Twas Mary the Maiden weeping cried:
    "Come forth, O Mother dear!"
'Twas Mary the Mother answered, "Nay!
    Go thou and leave me here!

"Go forth, go forth, and on your head
    All peace and blessing be,
But leave me here with the little Son
    I nurst upon my knee!

"There's room here at thy side, my Son,
    There's room here with thee,
And O to hold thee in my arms
    Is more than Heaven to me!

"And thou shalt sleep, and calm as thine
    My own deep sleep shall be!
For ever and for evermore
    I'll rest, my Son, with thee!"

They have led her forth from the lonesome place,
    Despite her woeful moan,
They have closed the mouth of the Sepulchre
    And sealed it with a stone;

And down the hill to Jerusalem
    They pass, but leave the three—
There is Mary the Mother, and Mary the Maiden,
    And Mary of Bethany.

'Twas Mary the dark-eyed Maiden
    First dried her weeping eyes:
"O Mother dear, we will keep watch here,
    For lo! he will arise!

"Master and Lord of men was he,
  And he will wake again,—
Yea ere he died he prophesied
  That he would rise and reign!

"He is not dead, but only sleeps,
  And soon shall rule again—
O Mother dear, we'll keep watch here,
  Till he doth rise and reign!"

'Twas Mary the Mother answered not,
  But sat like a frozen thing,
Her dim dark eyes on the door o' the Tomb,
  Vacant and famishing.

* * *

The first night they sat waiting there
    The great Deep thunder'd loud,
And the lightning Snakes crept in and out
    Their soot-black caves of cloud;

The next night they sat waiting there
    Came Silence strange and chill,
And the stars hung watching out of heaven,
    And the heart o' the world stood still;

The third night they sat waiting there
    The winds began to cry,
And a cold snow fell from the frozen stars,
    And the Spirit of Death went by!

'Twas Mary the woeful Mother
    Rose to her feet and said:
" The gate of the Tomb is sealéd fast,
    And the Light of the world hath fled.

"Never again shall the man my Son
   Brighten the night or the day—
The soul of a man is the breath of a mouth,
   And lo! it passeth away!

"And its oh, for the kiss of his mouth,
   And the touch of his hand,—aye me!
My day is dark, for the Lord my God
   Hath taken my child from me!

"And its oh, for his long long sleep,
   Alone in a lonely place,—
My Son is dead, for the wrath of the Lord
   Hath fallen and hidden his face.

"O had ye left me lying there,
   At his side or at his feet,
In peace, in peace, like a fount that falls,
   My heart has ceased to beat!"

Then Mary, the gentle Maiden,
   Answer'd her cry and said:
"Wait on, wait yet, for a heavenly sign
   That our Lord is quick, not dead!"

'Twas Mary the woeful Mother
  Stood up and rent her hair:
"Woe worth the day that I was born
  Or ever a son did bear!

"How shall the hand of a mortal
  Gather the sheaves of the Lord?
The hand of a man is ashes and dust,
  God's hand is fire and a sword!

"How shall the seed of a woman
  Master Euroclydon?
A woman's seed is as thistlebloom,
  And lo, with a breath 'tis gone!

"My son was fair as a lily,
  His hair was of golden sheen,
But the lilies of Sharon perish
  When the winds of the Lord blow keen!

"What man shall stand in the whirlwind
  Where only the Lord may stand?
The feet of the Lord are on the Dead,
  And the Quick blow round like sand!"

THE BALLAD OF MARY THE MOTHER

'Twas Mary the woeful Mother
   Crept down from Calvary,
Held up by Mary the Maiden
   And Mary of Bethany;

And over the hill the Dawn's bright feet
   Plash'd in the Night's cold springs,
And a lark rose, shaking the drops o' pearl
   From the tips of his dewy wings;

And the heart of the world throb'd deep and strong
   As on Creation's Day,
And the skies that roof the happy earth
   Were as blue and as far away!

* * *

Shepherd dear, the winds blow cold,
'Tis dark, so dark, on the wintry wold,—
Waken and gather thy flocks to fold!

Over the stormy hills they roam,
Feebly crying they go and come,
With never a Shepherd to help them home.

Shepherd dear, ere the day was done,
Around thy feet in the summer sun
They flock'd, and were counted one by one;

Thy white hands blest them, Shepherd dear,
And thy voice said sweetly: "Be of cheer!
The fold is open, and I am here."

Now, alas! the light hath fled,
The heavens are starless overhead,—
We listen still for thy voice, thy tread.

So cold, so still, this wintertide,
Thou sleepest, who wast once their guide,—
Thy crook lies broken at thy side.

The cold snow falls, the shrill winds cry,
The flocks are scatter'd, they droop and die,
And there's never a star in the wintry sky.

Alas! thou dost not see or hear!
In the frozen sheepfold, Shepherd dear,
Thou sleepest on, while we weep in fear.

Shepherd, Shepherd, the winds blow cold!
'Tis dark, so dark, on the wintry wold,—
Waken, and gather thy flocks to fold.

AD MADONNAM.

AD MADONNAM.

I.

If I could worship in these Shrines at all,
Methinks that 'twould be yonder, where I see
The Holy Mother fair and virginal
Holding the radiant Child upon her knee:
For Rome, eternal foe of all things free,
Still quick tho' stretch'd out cold 'neath Peter's
      pall,
By this one gift of grace redeems her fall
And makes amends to poor Humanity.
Madonna, pure as mortal mothers are,
Type of them all, for ever calm and good,
Over thy Son thou shinest like a star
While at thy milky breasts his mouth finds food . . .
Holiest and best of all things, holier far
Than Godhead, is eternal Motherhood!

II.

Nineteen sad centuries have passed away,
Madonna, since this Man thy Son was slain,

Since pillow'd on thy breast thy dead child lay
Nor heard thy moan of deep despair and pain :
So long! and all earth's tears have fallen in vain
Upon the grave that covereth that sweet clay—
Thou, too, didst cease to watch and plead and
      pray,
And slept at last never to wake again.
Best of all living creatures, thou alone
Whom God Himself had chosen (saith the
      Screed!)
Thou, Virgin of the Lily, must have known
If he, thy Son, was Son of God indeed;
Yet thou ('tis written) didst that claim disown,
Denying godhead to this Man, thy Seed!

III.

"*His Mother and his Brethren stood without
And waited!*" Ah, poor Mother, full of tears
While men believed and gladden'd, *thou* couldst
      doubt
And to that cry of godhead close thine ears!
Thro' the dark cloud of those forgotten years
I hear thee moaning yet, ring'd roundabout
With maniac faces, while the madmen shout

And high 'gainst Heaven the crimson Cross
    appears.
Mother of God! and yet thou couldst deny
In thine excess of love the Godlike claim!
Chosen of God,—yet thy despairing cry
Rose up to God in passionate grief and shame,
While, wrapt in kingly robes thy Son went by,
Nor answer'd when thy lips did breathe his
    name!

IV.

His face was raised to Heaven, not turn'd to thee,
While thou didst call him back from that mad
    quest;
Taught by thy Mother's heart, thine eyes could see
The piteous end of his divine unrest. . . .
Ah, well, God heard thy cry, and on thy breast
Again he sleeping lay, and thou and he,
United at God's feet, eternally
Abide in peace, of all things last and best. . . .
And yet, God knows! We know not! Wherefore,
    then,
The weary strife, the fret that ceaseth never,
Wherefore the witless want which maddeneth men,

The cruel sleepless quest, the long endeavour,
If, having waken'd once, we sleep again,
And lose our heritage of Love for ever?

V.

Our heritage of Love! . . Life and not Death,
Light and not Night, we seek from age to age;
The Spirit thou hast kindled with thy breath
To serve thee, Lord of Life, demands its wage!
Amid Thy tempests that for ever rage,
Man at thy conjuration travailleth:
" I did not crave to be, O God!" (he saith)
" But since I am, give me my heritage!
What thou hast quicken'd, what thy power hath
    taught
To serve thee through all moods of doubt and
    fear,—
The mystic mood that flashes back thy Thought,
The love that seeks thy Heaven, and finds it
    here,—
These are thy works, and what thy hand hath
    wrought
Claims service still, from sleepless year to year!"

VI.

And yet, alas, the ways of God are dark,
His purpose hid, His will a mystery,—
No sign or voice that man may see or hark
Hath ever broke His Law's Eternity.
A little space we strive, then cease to be,
A day we smile, and then lie stiff and stark,
Forgotten 'neath the dust with none to mark,
Silent, Madonna, like thy Son and thee!
God gave no answer to our brother's prayer,
The empty Heavens echoed back his cry;
He fainted 'neath the load we all must bear
That bitter day they led him forth to die,—
"Father," he cried, in darkness and despair,
And drank the Cup no hand hath yet put by!

VII.

Gentle and loving was this Man, thy Seed,
And innocent as any lamb at play,
For all the woes of man his heart did bleed,
Yea, till the wrath of God made dark his day,
Till with the whole world's woe his soul grew grey.
As radiant as the morning was his creed:
To heal the sick, to succour folk in need,

To bless the poor and wipe their tears away . . .
Then, groping darkly, maddening in his place,
Vainly he sought to grasp what none may find,—
For never tongue can speak or eye may trace
The Mystery God keeps dark from humankind,
And he who seeks to front God face to face
Is, by that Sun of Wonder, stricken blind!

VIII.

And lo! the issue! Of that loving Word
Thy dear one spoke, a multitudinous moan!
Not peace thy Son hath sent us, but a Sword
Shapen cross-wise, that flames from zone to zone!
And still the weary generations groan,
And still the vials of God's wrath are poured
On innocent and guilty, and the Lord
Veileth the very footstool of His Throne!
And unto every man, as to thy Son,
Cometh, at last, the same dark dread and doom—
All that our hands have wrought, our prayers have
      won,
Endeth with him in utterness of gloom,
Our brief day endeth, and our Dream is done,
And lo! the woven shroud, the opening tomb!

IX.

Patient Madonna, with the heavenly eyes,
Not upward bent, but downward on thy Child,—
Within thy open arms is Paradise
Happy and innocent and undefiled !
Smile thus, as many a mother sweet hath smiled,
Forgetful of that Shadow in the skies,—
Hushing the whole worlds' woe, and all the wild
Tumult of Nature, in thine Infant's cries ;
And there, beneath that ever-loving gaze,
Eternal Child, find peace and calm at last !
Deaf to thy passion, heedless of thy praise,
God dwelt afar off in the empty Vast,
But thou returnedest, after many days,
Unto the Heaven whence thy feet had passed !

* * *

I.

And O Madonna mine ! O dear grey-hair'd
    Mother, of human mothers first and best,
All that my soul hath sought, my dream hath dared,
    All that my youth and hope thought goodliest,
Depart, and leave me crying for thy breast !
    A child again, I see thy bosom bared,
And, lo ! I falter to the place prepared
    Where, after life's long fever, I may rest !
This gift alone, when the long day is done,
    I ask from Him who holds all gifts in store,—
After the weary battle, lost or won,
    To find thy love and blessing as before,
To be again thy little helpless son,
    And feel thy dear arms round me evermore !

II.

Thou sleepest, Dear !—and yet a little space
    I stir above thee, waiting for a sign :
Colder than coldest marble is thy face,
    Shut are thine eyes, I cannot see them shine ;

But thou wilt waken! and thine arms will twine
 Around me, in the dark and narrow place
Where thou art lying, and again God's grace
 And blessing will be on us, Mother mine!
My hair is gray like yours, my faltering feet
 Are weary, and my heart grows chill and cold,
Faint is the prayer my feeble lips repeat,
 Sad is the soul that once was bright and bold,
But when at last thou wakenest, smiling sweet,
 I'll be thy child again, not worn and old.

A CATECHISM.

A CATECHISM.

What is thy Name?

ROBERT BUCHANAN.

Who Gave thee that name?

Those from whose seed I grew:
He from whose loins I sprang, she in whose warm
Womb I grew shapen into flesh and form,—
Whereby I first did crawl, then walked upright,
A child, inheritor of Life and Light.

What did thy Father and Mother then for thee?

Three things they swore: firstly, to shelter me
From all things evil, teaching me to find,
Through love for them, due love for all Mankind;
Next, that through that first faith, made ripe and
      good
Through human motherhood and fatherhood,
My soul should learn to apprehend and know

The Parentage Divine whence all things flow;
Lastly, that, walking all my nights and days
In love and reverence, I should learn God's ways
And His commandments. These things in my
    name,
They promised and fulfill'd, until I came
To full estate of all Life's joys and woes;
And as the measure of my love for those
Who first made Earth a happy dwelling place,
And ring'd me round with offices of grace,
So may my love for all things measured be
Now and for ever, through Eternity.

*Dost thou still think that thou art bound in right
To keep those pledges?*

                      Yea, and morn and night
I keep them; if I stumble unawares,
The fault is on my head, and not on theirs
Who hold me dear for ever in their sight,
And turn'd my face to Heaven, to feel the Light.

Rehearse the articles of thy belief.

I do believe in God, supreme and chief
Of all things, first and last;—whose works proclaim

His glory, and the glories of His name;
I do believe in all the gods that shine
Beneath Him, humanized for eyes like mine
To images of loveliness divine;
I do believe that through my Father in Heaven
My sins (if Sin could be) would be forgiven,
And that, though Death for ever passes by,
Whate'er hath come to life can never die.

Thou saidst " If Sin could be ? "

      If Sin be blent
Into my nature as its element,
Then 'tis my God's as surely as 'tis mine;
But since I know my Father is Divine,
I know that all which seemeth Sin in me
Is but an image and a mystery.

Who is the God of Earth and Sea and Sky,
All-living and all-knowing ?

         He is I;
Impersonal in all that seems to be,
He first and last grew personal in me;
His inward essence shines behind these eyes;
His outer form in all they recognise.

Hath He no Being, then, apart from thee?

None.

Yet abideth through Eternity?

As *I* abide.

Yet is He Lord of Death?

Yea, and if *I* should perish, perisheth.

Is He not more than thou?

      He is the Whole
Of which I am the part, yet this my Soul
Is He, and surely through this sight of mine
He sees Himself and knows Himself Divine.

Now, name His attributes?

      They have but one name,—
Love, which embracing all things grows the same
As that it contemplates.

Lov'st thou the Lord?

Nay; tho' I bow before His will and word.

How doth He manifest Himself?

> In me,
> And in mine other self, Humanity.

Name the Commandments!

> Ten. Thou shalt have one
> God, and one only (may His will be done!)
> Thou shalt not fashion graven images
> Of Him, or any other, and to these
> Give prayer or praise; nor shall thy faith be priced
> By any priest of Christ or Antichrist,
> In any Temple or in any Fane;
> Thou shalt not take the Name of God in vain.
> All days shalt thou keep holy, pure and blest,
> Six shalt thou labour, on the seventh rest,
> But every day shall as a Sabbath be
> Of heavenly hope and love and charity.
> Honour thy father and thy mother,—not
> That God may lengthen and make bright thy lot,
> But that the love thou bearest them may spring
> Fountain-like to refresh each living thing
> Which lives and loves like thee. Slay not at
>   all,—
> Neither to feed thy wrath, nor at the call

Of nations lusting in accursèd strife,
Nor to appease the Law's black lust for life;
But take the murderer by the hand, and bring
Pity and mercy for his comforting.
Tho' thou must never an Adulterer be,
Deem not the deed of kind Adultery,
But reverence that function which keeps fair
The Earth, the Sea, the Ether, and the Air,
And peopling countless worlds with lives like
    thine,
Maketh all Nature fruitful and divine;
For as thou dost despise thy flesh and frame
Shalt thou despise the Lord thro' whom they
    came,
And if one act of these thou deemest base
Thou spittest in the Fountain of all Grace.
Thou shalt not steal, nor any lie sustain
Against thy neighbour; covet not his gain,
His wife, or ought that's his to have and hold,
For robbing him, thou rob'st thyself tenfold!

What dost thou learn from these Commandments?

                                        Love
For things around me, and for things above

Worship and reverence; hate of deeds that sin
Against the living God who dwells within
This Temple of my life; obedience
To that celestial Light which issues thence.

*Swearest thou to renounce, reject, and shun
The Flesh and all the lusts thereof?*

>   Not one;
For these are of the godhead, which is I,
And if this Flesh could pass, this Soul must die.

*Shall not the Flesh dissolve and disappear?
Shall not this Body which surrounds thee here
Pass into nothingness?*

>   Never, since 'tis made
Of God's own substance, which can never fade.

Dost thou believe in Jesus Christ, God's Son?

In Him, and in my Brethren every one:
The child of Mary who was crucified,
The gods of Hellas fair and radiant-eyed,
Brahm, Balder, Guatama, and Mahomet,
All who have pledged their gains to pay my debt
Of sorrows,—all who through this world of dream

Breathe mystery and ecstasy supreme;
The greater and the less: the wise, the good,
Inheritors of Nature's godlike mood;
In these I do believe eternally,
Knowing them deathless, like the God in *me*.

How many sacraments hath God ordained
Whereby the strength of man may be sustained?

None; since all sacraments in Man are blent,
And I myself am daily sacrament.

Dost thou not realise that, being base,
Thou art lost for ever, if no saving grace
Were sent in pity out of yonder sky?
Dost thou not know that, answering man's cry
For help and aid, thy God who is Divine
Put on a human likeness such as thine,—
Knew all thy doubts and fears, was foully slain,
Died, rose a space, and shall arise again?

Death cannot touch the Lord my God. I know
That in a dream of death long years ago
Mine Elder Brother beautiful and fair
Inherited life's sorrow and despair,
And being weary of the garish day

Died, blessing me.   He hath not passed away,
But filling all the world with his sweet breath
Walks, watch'd by two pale Angels, Sleep and
 Death.

Dost thou not in thine inmost heart believe,
Despite the lies which faithless sophists weave,
In Holy Church?

     All Churches, great or small !
But most, that roof'd with blue celestial,
And fairer far than Temples built by hands,
Which, while all others fall, survives and stands !
More, I believe in Hell, and hope for Heaven !
Yea, also, that my fears may be forgiven,
And that this Body shall arise again
To Light and Everlasting Life.   AMEN.

ANTIPHONES.

ANTIPHONES.

I.
THE LOVE OF GOD.

How can I love Thee, God that madeth me?
    Who saith he loves Thee, lies!
Behold him, mouthing on his bended knee,
    Upgazing to the skies!

Thy works, thy wonders, thine Omnipotence?
    Shall these awake my love?
Nay, these are only phantoms of the sense
    Whereby I live and move!

Thy mercies and thy gifts?—thy large delight
    In making living things?
Love is not born of any token bright
    Imperial Nature brings.

I love my fellow men, I love this hound
    Who gently licks my hand,
I love the land around me, and the sound
    Of children in the land.

But *Thee*? I love not Thee!—Stoop down, come
    near
  To me whom thou hast made,
Then I may know Thee close, and hold Thee
    dear,—
  But now I shrink afraid.

There's never a helpless thing surrounding me,
  No timid bird or beast,
I love not better far, O God, than Thee,
  Tho' Thou be first, these least.

I love the maid I woo, the mother whose touch
  I feel upon my brow,
The friend who grips my hand!—for these are such
  As I, and not as Thou.

Thou Vision of my Thought! Thou Mystery
  Of which men preach and rave!
I would not look, if Heaven held only *Thee*,
  One foot beyond the grave!

I seek the gentle ones who once were near,
  Not Thee, O Light above,—
I crave for all who learn'd to love me here
  And whom I learn'd to love!

Out of thy Darkness to this Light I came,
  Thro' whim or wish of thine,
O Miracle! O God Unknown! O Name
  Eternal and Divine!

And since Thy glory fills these nights and days
  That are so fugitive,
I give thee thanks, O God, I give thee praise,
  But love I cannot give!

II.
CONTRA CHRISTUM.

No Mediator, none! If thou art God,
  Thy torments were self-wrought;
If thou wast Man, despised and undertrod,
  Thy sorrows teach me nought.

I look within, and find my godhead *there*,
  Not yonder on the Cross;
Sharer of my soul's doubt, my heart's despair,
  My daily gain and loss.

How shouldst thou mediate for me and mine
   Who art thyself not free?
If thou thyself wast deathless and Divine,
   What part hast thou with *me*?

If thou art but the Son, and like the rest
   Fell slain before God's Throne,
Then will I love thee (lo! my hand is prest,
   Dear Comrade, in thine own!)

But if thou art the Father in disguise,
   I snatch my hand away—
Back to thy realm, back to thy silent skies,—
   I'll wait thy Judgment Day!

I search within, I find my one God still.
   What answereth He? "Had *I*
Been God all powerful, fashioning to my will
   All things that creep or fly,

"*I* had not built their glory or their gain
   On endless suffering,
I had not blent my Godhead with the pain
   Of any living thing."

Can the all Powerful be all Pitiful?
   The All-cruel be All-kind?
If this be so, then thou, my God, art null,
   Then thou, my Soul, art blind!

No Mediator, then! Soul of my Soul,
   God of my Thought, rest free:
Sure of myself while the long ages roll,
   I turn in peace to *Thee*.

III.

MY ENEMY.

Like to a Leper clings this man to me,
   I strike at him in vain;
My soul is haunted by mine enemy
   In endless forms of pain.

I would forget him, turning in delight
   To those my soul holds dear.
I cannot. Like my shadow, day and night,
   Mine enemy is here.

My very being, blighted with his breath,
   Droops like a thing forlorn,
Yea, with his presence, dim and dread as Death,
   My living force is worn.

I scorn him as the dust beneath my feet,
   I curse him loud or low—
God hears me yonder on His Judgment Seat,
   And yet he doth not go.

Yea, even more firmly than the first and best
   Of mortals loved by me,
Clingeth with fierce hands on my wounded
     breast,
   This man, mine enemy!

Sometimes, when fiercely struggling throat to
     throat,
   Like snakes that intertwine,
Our eyes meet, and within his eyes I note
   An agony like mine.

Sometimes, when God doth beckon from his
     skies
   And bids me climb or soar,
I see great tear-drops in the hated eyes
   That mock me ever more.

And now I know that neither I nor he
   Can ever part at all,—
If I arise, I lift mine enemy,
   And if he falls, I fall!

Nay, then, we two must down or upward move
   With the like end and aim,—
The links of Hate are as the links of Love,
   Nay (Nature saith) the same!

The same? Nay then, I hold mine enemy
   Too near for hate or scorn,
For what I hate in him is born of me,—
   Like his own hate, self-born.

At last I pray for him, and praying know
   That he and I are one,—
United at God's feet we fall, and lo!
   Our foolish strife is done!

IV.

RESURRECTION.

Scorner of Flesh, thou who wouldst plunge in
　　gloom
　　This radiant thing God made,
What shall abide if this should cease to bloom,
　　This Flesh Divine should fade?

The Soul? A Flower of which this Flesh is seed?
　　Nay, Flesh and Soul are one!
Thou who wouldst part this one in twain, take
　　　　heed,
　　Lest all should be undone!

This eye of Flesh, to see and apprehend,
　　Is thy Soul's eye! This clay,
That adumbrates thy Soul, shall find no end
　　Till that, too, fades away!

Lo, lying with a lily in her hand,
　　Thy dear one slumbereth,—
Yet on a day she shall arise and stand
　　Smiling on vanquish'd Death.

All Flesh, all Form, all that was pure and fair
   Here on Life's crowded road,
She shall arise,—nay, not one little hair
   Shall pass away, saith God!

All that was beautiful, all thine eyes and sense
   Saw beautiful and whole,
The Form, the Flesh, no part shall vanish hence,
   Since these things are the Soul!

Nought that is beautiful can die,—no form
   That once grew fair can fade,—
This flesh shall still be radiant, sweet, and warm,
   Form of the soul God made!

From the unconscious to the conscious life
   Man hath emerged, to know
Self-knowledge, Sight, victorious o'er the strife
   Of Nature's ebb and flow.

The day God can divide this life in twain
   Its length of day is done,
But both, be sure, will rise and live again,
   If Flesh and Soul are one!

V.

NATURE.

Nought is so sure as this, that Nature strives
    Reckless of human pain,
That on the hecatomb of slaughtered lives
    She looks with large disdain.

Canst thou appease her hunger? For a space,
    But surely not for long;—
She strews Life's Deep with wreckage of our race
    For she alone is strong.

Behind her footsteps crawl Calamity,
    Sorrow, Disease, and Death;
And yet she shareth in the agony
    Of these, who are her breath.

Gladsome and beautiful, divinely fair,
    Eager to blight or bless,
She carries in her heart all life's despair,
    Yet still is pitiless.

How then escape her? Summon to thine aid
  Thy God, all gods that be,—
Inexorable, silent, undismayed,
  She smiles on them and thee.

Fringe of her raiment, dewdrops on her feet,
  Gleams of her own surmise,
Thy gods go with her, fading as they meet
  The flashing of her eyes.

Dying yet deathless, changeful yet unchanged,
  Still here, though all are gone,
All Love, all Hate, avenging and avenged,
  She passeth slowly on.

Yet be of comfort,—let her wend her way!
  Watch as she goeth by!
The power which slayeth all things cannot slay
  Herself,—who cannot die;

And *thou*, my Soul, art deathless, being part
  Of her who is Divine,—
Pulse of that great and ever-beating Heart,
  Its length of life is thine!

Destroying all things, she destroyeth nought,
  (Wherefore, be comforted!)
For if her life could fail within thy thought,
  She would herself be dead!

L'ENVOI.

L'ENVOI.

    Think not that I blaspheme
Because I worship not this God of thine;
Because I bend not, either in deed or dream,
        To that dread Force Divine.

    Atheist thou callest me,
'Aθεòς, he who stands apart from God,
While priests and poets name Him fearfully
        And tremble at His nod!

    Poets and priests have lied
From immemorial Time, and still they lie;
Close to the ground they watch, dull-soul'd, dull-
        eyed,
        The Lord of Hosts go by!

    Not thus in far off days
The Titan stood, fronting the stars and sun—
Erect he watch'd, with neither prayer nor praise,
        The inevitable One!

’Αθεὸς, too, was he
Who everywhere the Soul of Pity saw—
The God he prayed to, yonder in Galilee,
    Was *not* your God of Law!

He dream'd as atheists do
Of Love that triumphs on, tho' undertrod;
He worshipt not the gloomy God o' the Jew,
    Nor even Nature's God!

The Law, the Might, the Lord,
Won not the worship of the Crucified,—
Murmuring another name, a gentler word,
    The last Great Dreamer died.

Alas he could not heal
The woes of Nature, or subdue her strife,—
But in sublime revolt he made men feel
    The piteousness of Life! . . .

It is not reverence
To kneel in Temples priests and slaves upraise:
The Law which sweeps us hither and sweeps us
    hence
    Heeds not our prayer or praise.

It is not blasphemy
To front, Prometheus-like, Eternal Fate!
The God to whom your priests now bend the knee
Left Jesus desolate!

So died he, ἀθεὸς,
Seeking in vain to break the Tyrant's rod;
Tormented, like Prometheus, on his Cross,
By all the slaves of God!

PROSE NOTE.

PROSE NOTE.

THE ATHEISM OF JESUS.

I.

I HAVE thought myself justified, while trying to realise how Jesus of Nazareth may have struck a contemporary, in using as my dramatic mouthpiece his own Mother, the wife of Joseph the Carpenter. All the phases of my conception can be supported, if necessary, by the existing Christian documents; and if they could not be so supported, they are still justifiable, since the imagination of a modern Poet is fully as reliable as the imagination of a mediæval Monk.

Goethe, in his old age, foresaw the time when Christianity might become a *subject* for Poetry; a subject, that is to say, to be treated without reference of any kind to existing dogma or superstition. Thanks to modern scientific thought, the time has come sooner than was anticipated. We have reached the 'vantage-ground where the story of Jesus can be taken out of the realm of Supernaturalism and viewed humanly, in the domain of sympathetic Art. To even so late an observer as Rénan such a point of view was difficult, not to say impossible. Now, for the first time, human Science has actually uttered its fiat and written it on the rock. That fiat is, "The Law of God is *never* broken! Whosoever professes to break the Eternal Order is ignorant of the Divine Method— the true Atheist—$\mathring{a}\theta\epsilon\grave{o}s$, apart from God." It seems a paradox to say so, but in this respect—ignorance of the Divine Law, assumption of powers to break it or suspend it—Jesus of Nazareth was an unbeliever, perhaps the most audacious unbeliever who has ever lived.

He led the war against Nature, against the God of Nature, and that unhappy war is not over yet. But he, the new Prometheus, urging on his legions of despairing Titans, adopted a new system of attack—he assumed that the God of Nature *did not exist;* and he substituted in his imagination a new Personality, his own. History has furnished the answer to his pretensions, and the God of Nature, the great unknown God who is at once the master and servant of His own inexorable Will, has conquered all along the line. God reigns — Jesus and the Titans have failed; and their failure has deluged the world with innocent blood.

In saying so much, I do not wish to infer that my sympathy is with the Conqueror. No; it is with the fallen Atheists, not with the ever-victorious Deity whom they have one by one denied; with Prometheus, with Jesus; with the Dreamers who would fain dry the weeping eyes of men. Though they turn from the living God and substitute the gentle Phantom of their own desire; though they utter a promise which is ever broken, assume a hope which can never be realised: they are still, in the sweetest and surest meaning of the word, our Brethren, and we forgive them their sins against the eternal Law, because we, too, would fain dream as they do. Alas, that the time should come when we must dream no more!

Meantime, let it be clearly understood that the Poets have ever been on the losing side, on the side, that is to say, of Jesus and the Titan-Dreamers: and hence the proof of a Poet is still to be found in his temperamental antagonism to the God of Nature.

II.

In what he chooses to call "A Modern View of Jesus Christ," and which he describes as a picture "in no way concerned with the disputed question of the Divinity of Jesus," Mr. G. B. Crozier, author of a work on "Civilisation and Progress," betrays the usual indifference to logic which seems to beset all men who trim and tinker the bewildering popular religion. His account of the moral evolution of Jesus, from the period when the Nazarene postulated a Judaic God of Justice, until the period when he postulated instead a cosmic God of Love, is framed in the familiar manner of light-hearted amateur historians and light-headed Broad-Church divines. In the discussion of any other subject, save this creed of formulas and cobwebs, a writer of Mr. Crozier's intelligence would first marshall his facts and then frame his theories; but the invariable method of Christian theologians and historians is to frame the theories first, and then marshall the facts to support them. "For when John," says Mr. Crozier, "sent his disciples to ask Jesus whether or not he were really the Messiah, Jesus *simply* (*sic!*) said, 'Go and show John these things which ye hear and see,—the blind receive their sight, the lame walk, the lepers are cleansed and the deaf hear, the dead are raised up, and the poor have the Gospel preached to them.'" "Indeed," adds Mr. Crozier, "the more he, Jesus, pondered, the more he was convinced that the only kind of Messiah that could possibly be sent by a God of Love must be a comforter of the poor and weak, the lowly, the broken-hearted: a healer of the deaf, the lame, the blind, etc." In other words, the only possible method by which a God of Love could reveal Himself to his creatures would be the method adopted by every God of Wrath,—the breaking of His own laws, the revelation of His own caprice,—the method, in short, of popular Thaumaturgy! Thus a fairly intelligent and eclectic writer, beset by the insincerity of his hopeless subject, begins by telling us that his picture has nothing to do with the question of the Divinity of Jesus, and then accepts *en bloc* the signs, portents, and miracles which, if established by rational evidence, would put the *quæstio vexata* at rest for ever!

In this connection, therefore, it is necessary to repeat with emphasis that it is on the truth or falsehood of the supernatural pretension that the *moral* character of Jesus must finally stand or fall. It was by Miracles that he attested his divine sovereignty; it was by Miracles that he won his first following; it was by Miracles that he proclaimed himself the Son of God; and without the historical belief in the Miracles Christianity would have died a natural death in its first infancy. It is not, indeed, a creed of Love which has fascinated Humanity. "God is Love," cried Jesus; "and my *proof* that God is Love is this,—I can heal the sick, and I can raise the dead." The whole question, therefore, is reduced to one of facts, of proof. If we can believe that Jesus raised the dead, if we can even believe that any dead man since the world's beginning has slipt his shroud and arisen, then we need not hesitate for a moment in accepting the pretensions of Christianity. If, on the other hand, we believe that the eternal Law is *never* broken, we need not pause to consider the moral character of Jesus. We may accept him (as we are bound to do) as a man of a supremely noble and loving nature, we may even believe that, in the assumption of supernatural power, he was merely self-deluded, not dishonest; but we cannot bow down before him as either the incarnate God or even the wisest of men.

The fit and only platform to discuss and examine this religion, this many coloured kaleidoscope which men call Christianity, is, consequently, our own experience of human and natural phenomena. In the light or darkness of our own dwellings, in the silence of our own thoughts, in the record of all we have seen, known, and felt, in the presence of our own beloved ones, and by the sleeping places of our own dead, we have to ask ourselves— has the God of Love, in whom we may otherwise believe, ever attested his being by any interruption of his own laws? Has he not, on the contrary, sealed up the eyes of the blind, left the leper to die of his disease, forborne to disturb, or even break, the sleep of Death? If it is borne in upon us, every day we live, that the laws of life are *never* broken, and that God has never vouchsafed us a sign, even a glimmer, of His personal presence, what shall we say of the folly, or the insanity, of the great Atheists who have perished miserably in the assumption of miraculous or God-like power?

"Grant, indeed," says the bewildered sentimentalist, "that the proof has failed, that no miracle was ever wrought, does not the divine spirit of Jesus remain secure to pervade creation?" By no means. The spirit was that of a deluded sceptic who aspired to break, and who misinterpreted, the laws of God, and who perished, of necessity, like a fly on the wheel. How then, it is asked, has Christianity itself emerged to save and gladden the souls of men? Here, again, our opponents are arguing in a circle, for the religion of Jesus has never really triumphed at all, except in the area of priestly politics and popular superstition. Our time has been wasted, we have been made the sport of a kindly thaumaturgist, for nearly nineteen hundred years.

Meantime we have constructed, out of the débris of

historical documents, an ideal Jesus, a fanciful and fictitious Son of God. All the hope and despair of Humanity, the blood of the Martyrs, the visions of the Prophets, the dreams of the Poets, have nurtured this imaginary Messiah, who sums up in his nebulous person all that we mortals are, or hope to be. He heals no sick, he raises no dead, it is true; we begin to realise at last that he can never have done so; but Jesus, like Mesopotamia, is a blessed word, and we cling to it with fond tenacity.

In this poem, however, I at least acquit the Nazarene of his atheism—that is, I make him realise, after his momentary madness of supposed godhead, that the creature who endeavours to break the Divine Order must meet the Atheist's doom. Cruel and inexplicable as that Order is, it is absolute and inevitable. Humanity will never free itself from its chains by assuming *that they do not exist*. The true believer in God is the man who discovers and recognises His pitiless laws, from the first Law till the last. The true witness to God is the man who, much as he execrates the anarchy and cruelty of Nature, and as a consequence of the God of Nature, accepts things as they are and endeavours to lighten the burthen for his fellow-men. Jesus was a man of a beautiful temperament, carried beyond himself by a false and sentimental conception of the mechanism of Life. He uttered, no one so exquisitely, the human cry for a Divine Fatherhood. But unfortunately, he appealed to Nature for corroboration of his appeal. Nature never answered him; then as now, she kept God's secret.

R. B.

www.ingramcontent.com/pod-product-compliance
Lightning Source LLC
Chambersburg PA
CBHW030304170426
43202CB00009B/869